Journey Well, Little One

Sidney James

BookLeaf Publishing

India | USA | UK

Journey Well, Little One © 2022 Sidney James

All rights reserved.

No part of this publication may be reproduced, stored in a retrieval system, or transmitted, in any form or by any means, electronic, mechanical, photocopying, recording or otherwise, without the prior written permission of the presenters.

Sidney James asserts the moral right to be identified as author of this work.

Presentation by *BookLeaf Publishing*

Web: www.bookleafpub.com

E-mail: info@bookleafpub.com

ISBN: 9789357448055

First edition 2022

DEDICATION

To Spleen: Little Snail, thank you for climbing the mountain with me.

ACKNOWLEDGEMENT

It has been years and yet these immortal words by Kobayashi Issa have stayed true within my life:

Katasumuri
Soro soro nobore
Fuji no yama

O snail,
Climb Mt. Fuji
But slowly, slowly!

This book has been (as I have been) heavily influenced by this poem and without it I would not have been so inspired.

PREFACE

We are each on our own path. These paths are seemingly endless; filled with mountains and valleys, intersected with rivers, whole oceans, walls, and unknowns. Although we travel alone, ultimately our journey is together. Our path exists at the same time as others and may cross or align or become one path for a time. Without support how would we share our burdens or our successes? These poems are about the obstacles and the triumphs found in the steps towards good health but mostly they are about the journey. I am thankful for all of those who journey with me.

Slowly Climbing

Little One climb high
Climb the Rocky Mountain path
But slowly, slowly

Satisfaction

Little One rest now
This step is finished, well done
Be proud of yourself

Bad Days

Little One take heart
Each one of us has bad days
You will get better

Back On Track

Little One look far
See the forest through the trees
But honour each branch

Happy

Little One listen
Do you hear the sweet wind's song?
Be happy, happy

Sharing The Burden

Little One cheer up!
You have loved ones on your side
Please share the burden

Deception

Little One beware
Although this path seems easy
It will take hard work

Kindness

Little One be kind
To all, yourself and others
Then you'll always win

Seasons Turn

Little One things change
The you of today will not
Be here tomorrow

Hiding

Little One unmask
You don't need to hide yourself
Your truth is perfect

Fortis

Little One be brave
One life, one choice, one moment
Can create worlds

Darkness

Little One don't hate
Everything has a bright side
Darkness holds you back

Full Belly

Little One consume
Good food in healthy amounts
Nourish your body

A new reality

Little One daydream
Think up fantastic magic
Create and dream big

You Win

Little One well done
You woke up and tried again
Once more, keep going

You are worth it

Little One speak up
Your own opinions matter
Advocate for You

In sickness and in health

Little One heal well
Slowly, gently, quietly
You will become whole

Big Emotions

Little One please cry
Tears of all kinds should be shed
You are free to feel

Still progressing

Little One hold fast
Two steps forward one step back
Be kind to yourself

The Last Push

Little One look, there!
The summit is in our sights!
Just one last big push!

Slower still, but stronger

Little One step strong
Descend the Rocky Mountain
but slowly, slowly